Jump Rope Johnny and the Inspiring Mr. P

How One Teacher Forever Changed the Life of His Student

Andrew T. Dunne

Illustrations by Jeong Da Jeong

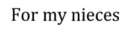
For my nieces

INTRODUCTION

When I was in fifth grade, the other students called me *Johnny Peter the Eater* because I was overweight.

I hated that nickname. Every time someone called me *Johnny Peter the Eater*, I smiled and laughed, but I really felt like crying.

Some really mean students would push me in the hallway and say, "Move out of the way fat boy".

The class I hated the most was physical education because I didn't like to exercise, and I was embarrassed to change my clothes in front of the other boys in the changing room.

During recess and lunch, the other kids played outside. They played soccer, basketball, tag, and tetherball.

I tried to play with them many times but no one ever wanted me to be on their team.

I was the kid who was always picked last for team sports.

The other kids would laugh at me because I moved slowly and I got out of breath so easily.

So, I preferred to be alone. I played computer games or games on my phone.

Then one day, a substitute teacher named Mr. P heard me crying in the computer room.

He entered the room and took a seat next to me.

That day, Mr. P would forever change my life.

CHAPTER 1

Meeting Mr. P

"Johnny, what's wrong?" Mr. P asked.

"Nothing", I said.

"Why aren't you outside playing with the other kids?"

"They don't like me, and they say I'm too fat and too slow to play with them".

"I'm sorry to hear that, Johnny. When I was a kid, I was overweight, too. I got teased all the time by my classmates. It made me sad".

Mr. P was in great shape, so I was surprised to hear he got teased for being overweight.

I said, "You were once fat. No way!
Really? I can't believe anyone would
ever tease you".

"Yes, Johnny. I was bullied almost
every day because of my weight".

"You were just like me".

"Yes, I was. And do you know what?"

"What?"

"I can help you", said Mr. P.

"You can?" I said with excitement.

"Yes, Johnny. I will share with you what I did to improve my situation. But first, let me ask you something about books".

"Books", I said, surprised. "Okay".

CHAPTER 2

Don't Judge a Book by its Cover

"I always see you carrying a book. You like to read, don't you?" asked Mr. P.

"Yes, I love reading. I read one book a week. I especially love fiction. Right now, I'm reading a book about a boy who is half-wolf and he falls in love with a girl who has magic powers".

"That's fantastic, Johnny. And when you go to the library or to the book store, do you sometimes choose to read one book instead of another book because of the way the cover looks?"

"Yeah, I do that all the time. I like book covers with a lot of colors and big letters".

"Why don't you like book covers that aren't colorful or that have small letters?"

"I don't know. I guess I think they look boring".

"Well, our bodies and the way we look are like a book cover", said Mr. P.

"They are?"

"Yes, Johnny. You see, just because someone is overweight doesn't mean they are a bad person. I have friends who are overweight and they are incredible people. But some kids might choose not to play with another kid because of the way they look and they might tease them, too. It's not nice, but it happens, unfortunately".

"That's right", I said.

Mr. P continued talking. "When I was in school, *Chicken Legs* was the nickname kids had for Bobby because he had thin legs. Zach was teased because of his hairy arms and called *Gorilla*. But do you know what?"

"What?"

"Even the popular kids sometimes got teased for how they looked".

"They did?" I asked, surprised.

"I remember when Lisa, who everyone thought was so beautiful, came to school with some pimples on her face and many of the students called her *Pizza Face*. And my friend Lauren, who was very pretty, was called *Giraffe* because she was the tallest in our class. But when she was in high school, Lauren became a model for fashion magazines".

"Oh, wow!" I said.

"Yes, Johnny, so you are not alone. Many people get teased and bullied for the way their bodies and faces look, even for the way they dress, as well as for the way they talk, walk, and laugh".

"You're right", I said. "So, why do people tease?"

"Well, sometimes friends tease each other. Sometimes people tease each other to have a laugh. But some people get satisfaction or pleasure from making other people feel bad. If someone teases you, they may be unhappy with something in their own lives. So, to make themselves feel better, they try to hurt you".

"I think I understand. Did your classmates have a mean nickname for you, Mr. P?"

"Oh, yes. Many of the kids at my school called me *Jelly-Belly*".

 "They did?"

"Yes".

"So, what did you do when they called you *Jelly-Belly*?"

"I usually laughed, but I felt like crying".

"That's what I do, too", I said.

He continued talking, "There's nothing wrong with being overweight if you are happy with the way you look and feel. But the heavier I got, I began to have problems".

"What kind of problems?" I asked.

"My knees and back hurt when I walked up stairs and it became harder to breathe".

"I know what you mean. I have the same problems".

"Well, during one summer vacation, I decided to change", said Mr. P. "I lost weight and the next school term, I was able to play sports more easily with the other kids during recess and lunch. The other kids also began to treat me differently. We even became friends".

"You even became friends", I said, surprised. "Really?"

"Yes".

"How did you lose weight?" I asked.

"I used this".

Mr. P opened his briefcase and took out a jump rope.

CHAPTER 3

Mr. P Jumps Rope

"Almost every day, I jump rope for 10 or 15 minutes, sometimes 30 or 40 minutes when I'm having a lot of fun", said Mr. P.

He then moved some tables to create space.

"Watch this, Johnny".

He jumped slowly to begin. Then he spun the rope faster and faster, and then he did tricks.

It was amazing. The jump rope and Mr. P's feet and hands were moving so fast. I couldn't believe it.

When he stopped jumping, he handed me the jump rope and said, "Here, you try".

"No way, I can't".

That's when Mr. P taught me a very important lesson.

CHAPTER 4

A Master was once a Beginner

Mr. P said, "You can't jump rope yet".

"Yet? What does that mean?"

"It means you can't do something right now, but with practice, you can learn".

"I'm confused".

"Let me try to explain. You like ice hockey, right?" asked Mr. P.

I guess he noticed that I wore ice hockey jerseys to school most days.

"Yeah, I love watching ice hockey", I said.

"Who is your favorite player?" asked Mr. P.

"Marcus David", I said with enthusiasm.

"Great choice! He is an ice hockey master".

"What is a master?" I asked.

"A master is someone who is excellent at doing something".

"Ah, I understand".

"Did you know that when he was about your age, Marcus David couldn't play ice hockey?" asked Mr. P.

"No way!" I said. "Are you sure?"

"Yes, I'm sure, Johnny. He began learning how to play when he was 10".

He paused, and then slowly said, "Every master started as a beginner".

"Every master started as a beginner", I repeated.

"That's right", Mr. P said. "Marcus David had to learn how to ice skate, stick handle, pass, and shoot. He had to practice a lot".

"He did?"

"Yes. And, so you see, Johnny, you can't jump rope right now because you haven't practiced. But if you practice and don't give up, you can learn".

"I can?"

"Yes, Johnny. But, it can take a long time to learn certain things. Learning can be challenging. When we are learning how to do something, we may make many mistakes".

"Did you make many mistakes when you were learning how to jump rope?" I asked.

"Every day", said Mr. P. "And do you know what?"

"What?"

He smiled and said, "I still make mistakes".

"You do?" I said, surprised.

"I certainly do, Johnny".

CHAPTER 5

Learning from Mistakes

"Making mistakes isn't fun", said Mr. P. "But it's often how we learn. When I make a mistake, I don't quit. I try again, and again, and again. When I make a mistake, I think about what I did wrong and how I can fix it the next time I try".

He then leaned forward and said, "People who win never quit and people who quit never win".

"People who win never quit and people who quit never win", I repeated.

I was a little confused. "What does quit mean?"

"To quit means to stop trying".

"I see. So, winners never stop practicing and people who never practice don't win. Right?"

"That's right! Excellent, Johnny".

Mr. P continued talking. "When I was learning how to jump rope, the rope kept hitting my feet and my legs. I jumped too high. I got tired very easily. Many days, I wanted to quit".

"You wanted to quit?"

"Yes. Many days I threw my jump rope on the ground because I was so frustrated".

"Frus….frus…frustrated", I said, finding it hard to pronounce the word.

"Yes, frustrated. You see, when we make mistakes, we can become angry at ourselves. We become frustrated because we feel like we can't learn or do something. We might even feel like we're stupid".

"Yes, when I play computer games, I sometimes get frustrated and mad at myself when I don't get high scores", I said.

"But do you stop playing?" asked Mr. P.

"No".

"Exactly", said Mr. P. "Everyone makes mistakes. What's important is what you do after you make a mistake. Do you quit or do you keep trying?"

"I should keep trying", I said.

"Yes, Johnny. When I was learning how to jump rope, I made so many mistakes, but I kept practicing and practicing. Then jumping rope became easier and easier".

"It did?"

"Yes, it did. But do you know what I did then?" asked Mr. P.

"No, what did you do?"

"I made jumping rope more challenging".

"What? You made it more challenging. Why? How?" I asked.

"I tried to learn difficult jump rope tricks like double unders and criss-crosses".

"Double unders and criss-crosses", I repeated. "What are they?"

"Watch this", said Mr. P.

Mr. P put out his hand, and so I gave him the jump rope.

He jumped once and spun the rope so fast that it went under his body two times before his feet touched the ground. That's called a double under.

Then he jumped again and this time he crossed the rope in front of his body. The next time he jumped, he uncrossed the rope. That's called a criss-cross.

"Awesome! Awesome!" I shouted. "How did you do that?"

"With lots and lots of practice, Johnny. When I started learning different jump rope tricks, I made so many mistakes".

"But you didn't quit", I said.

"That's right, Johnny. I never quit. That's the secret. If you want to learn how to jump rope or to learn something else, you have to practice, practice, practice. Don't give up".

"Don't give up", I repeated. "Okay".

"There were days when I felt like I was getting worse at jumping rope, but sometimes that happens just before you get better", said Mr. P.

"You sometimes got worse before you got better. I don't understand".

"Let me try to explain", said Mr. P.

"Okay".

"Well, Johnny, you enjoy computer games, right?"

"Yes".

"In your favorite computer game, does your character have a special tool?" asked Mr. P.

"Yes, he has a hammer, a knife, and a bow and arrow".

"Okay. How do you use the bow and arrow?" asked Mr. P.

CHAPTER 6

An Arrow is Pulled Backwards

"To shoot the arrow forward, first it has to be pulled backwards", I said.

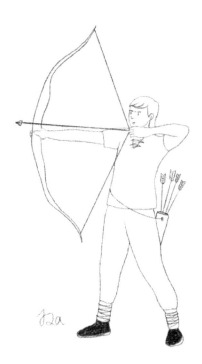

"So, before an arrow goes forward, first it must be pulled backwards. Is that right?" asked Mr. P.

"Yes".

"A similar thing can happen when we are trying to learn something", said Mr. P. "You see, Johnny, when we make mistakes, we might feel like we're going backwards or getting worse, but if we don't give up and we keep trying, soon we will get better. We will go forward like an arrow. Does that make sense?"

"Yes, it does".

"Great, Johnny".

CHAPTER 7

Be the Best You can Be

"Mr. P, are you the best jump roper in the world?" I asked.

Mr. P let out a big laugh.

"No, there are many people who are much better at jumping rope than me. But, that's okay. I don't have to be the best. I just have to try my best. I want to be the best that I can be. That's what's important, Johnny. Every day, I try to get a little better. I try to make small improvements each day. Some days, I get better. Some days, I don't get better. But I never give up. And, do you know what else?"

"What else?"

"The best jump ropers in the world make mistakes, too. Some days, they make so many mistakes that even they think they are not good".

"Really? They do?" I said, surprised.

"Yes. Even people who are the best at something sometimes think they are not good".

"Why?" I asked.

CHAPTER 8

We Judge Ourselves Harshly

"Well, it's hard to explain", said Mr. P. "But a strange thing about us humans is that our minds often try to tell us negative thoughts and make us feel worried or scared. Sometimes we think too much about the mistakes we make instead of about all the things we have done well and all the things we can do well in the future. For example, I remember when I was your age, and I got 47 questions correct on a science exam that I studied really hard for. There were 50 questions. Instead of being happy that I did really well, I was mad at myself for getting 3 questions wrong".

"I think I understand", I said. "We can learn from our mistakes, but we shouldn't only think about our mistakes. We have to remember and be proud of all the good things we have done and that we can do in the future if we work hard. Right?"

"Yes, that's right, Johnny".

Then he handed me the jump rope and said, "Here, you try".

"No, I can't".

"You can't yet, Johnny, but you will. Just try".

"How do I start?" I asked.

"Let me show you".

I gave Mr. P the jump rope. He put it behind his body. Then he moved his arms and hands to spin the rope. As the rope began to spin over his head, he bent his knees and jumped.

"Now, you try", he said while giving me the jump rope.

"No, I can't! I'm scared of hitting myself with the rope or tripping on the rope and falling down".

CHAPTER 9

Overcoming Fear

"I was scared the first time I tried jumping rope, too", said Mr. P. "It's normal to feel scared when you try something new. But one of the best ways to defeat fear is to try doing the thing that scares you. When you try, you realize the thing wasn't that scary".

"No, I can't jump rope. I'm scared".

"Did you know that your favorite ice hockey player Marcus David was scared when he tried to ice skate for the first time?" asked Mr. P.

"He was?" I said, surprised.

"Yes, he was. But each time he skated, he felt less and less afraid. If he never tried, he would never have learned to skate. He slipped and fell many times on the ice, but he kept getting up and kept trying".

Mr. P then gave me the jump rope.

Feeling inspired, I put the rope behind my legs. Next, I spun the rope over my head and jumped off the ground.

"Nuts", I shouted, as the rope got caught in my feet. "See, I can't do it. I failed. I'm a failure".

"Johnny, you are not a failure. You tried and you made a mistake. The important thing is that you tried. Does Marcus David score a goal every time he takes a shot?"

"No, he doesn't".

"When he misses a shot, does he quit? Does he stop taking shots?" asked Mr. P.

"No".

"Johnny, be like Marcus David".

He then pointed at the jump rope and said, "Try again".

I tried, but again the rope got caught in my feet.

"Good try, Johnny. That was better".

"It was?"

"Yes, it was. Try again. You can do it. I believe in you".

CHAPTER 10

Self-Belief

"Mr. P, you believe in me, really?"

"Yes, I believe in you, Johnny. I know that you can jump rope. But that's not what is important. What is important is that you believe in yourself. I want you to remember something".

"What do you want me to remember?" I asked.

"In life, you will meet many people who will tell you that you can't do something; that you aren't good enough. But, believe in yourself. If you work hard, you can accomplish great things. We can't control what other people say or what they do, but we can control how we behave. Do you understand?"

"Um, I think so. If someone tells me I'm not good at something, I don't have to believe them. If I practice, I can become good. Am I right?"

"Right! Excellent, Johnny. Now, try to jump rope again. This time, wait until the rope passes over your head before jumping".

"Okay, I will do that".

"But first, try this: close your eyes", said Mr. P.

"Why should I close my eyes?" I asked.

"It's called visualization".

"Vi…vi….what?"

"Visualization.   Vi-zhoo-uh-lie-zay-shin", said Mr. P, slowly.

CHAPTER 11

Imagine Yourself Doing Well

"Vi-zhoo-uh-lie-zay-shin", I repeated. "What is that?"

"Visualization means to imagine what you want to achieve".

"To imagine what I want to achieve", I repeated.

"Let's try together", said Mr. P.

"Okay, let's try".

"Close your eyes again".

I closed my eyes.

"Now, I want you to imagine yourself jumping over the rope", said Mr. P.

"Okay".

"No, don't open your eyes, Johnny. Keep your eyes closed but try to see yourself jumping over the rope. Wait for the rope to pass over your head before jumping".

"Yes! I'm doing it, Mr. P. I'm jumping rope in my mind".

"Good, Johnny. Now, open your eyes and try doing it for real".

"Okay, here I go".

I stepped over the rope so it was behind my legs. I then spun the rope using my wrists and arms and when the rope passed over my head, that's when I bent my knees and began to jump by pushing my toes into the ground.

This time I jumped over the rope. I was so happy.

"I did it, Mr. P. I did it! I really did it. Did you see?"

"I sure did. You did great. Well done, Johnny".

"That was so awesome!" I shouted.

He then said, "I want you to remember another thing".

"What do you want me to remember?"

CHAPTER 12

Strong People Help Others

"Johnny, when you first tried to jump over the rope, you made a mistake, right?"

"Right".

"And what did I do?" asked Mr. P. "Did I laugh at you or say mean things to you?"

"No, you didn't".

"I gave advice to help you. I didn't tease you or say you are bad at jumping rope. A weak person would do that. Weak people try to push other people down with their words. Strong people try to lift other people up with helpful words and advice".

"I thought a strong person is someone who has lots of muscles", I said.

"Yes, muscles can be a sign of strength", said Mr. P. "But being strong is not just about being able to lift a heavy object or push something heavy. We can lift people up by the way we behave".

"I think I understand", I said. "For example, if Marcus David gives advice to his teammate George Kelly, George will play better and then George will feel better about himself. Is that right?"

"That's right, Johnny. Very good! Also, because George Kelly will play better, that will help Marcus David play even better, too. If each player on the team plays well, the whole team plays better".

"I understand. That makes sense. Like, if my sister is sad, and I cheer her up, I will feel happier because my sister is happier, and then even our parents will feel happier".

"Yes, that's exactly right, Johnny. Fantastic example!"

"Similarly, if my sister does something well, I can be happy for her, and then when I do something well, she'll be happy for me", I said. "Right?"

"Right, Johnny. Awesome!"

I smiled and laughed because Mr. P was so happy and because he used the word awesome, which is one of my favorite words.

Then he asked me to jump rope again. But this time, he asked me to try jumping over the rope two times in a row.

"Two times in a row", I said, surprised. "Really?"

"Yes, let me show you".

I gave Mr. P the jump rope. He jumped over the rope. Then he jumped over the rope again.

"Now, you try", he said.

"Okay. Here I go".

I spun the rope and jumped over it. Then I spun it again and jumped over it.

"I did it, Mr. P. I jumped over the rope two times in a row. That was awesome!"

CHAPTER 13

You are Braver than You Think

"Well done, Johnny. Now, try to do three jumps in a row".

"Three jumps?"

"Yes. Three jumps in a row".

I jumped over the rope two times, but the rope hit my feet on the third spin.

"Oh no, I didn't do it", I said.

"That's okay. Try again", said Mr. P.

"I'm scared".

"For the next five seconds, Johnny, don't be scared. Be brave. You can do it".

This time, I did it. And I even jumped over the rope four extra times.

"Did you see that Mr. P? I jumped over the rope seven times in a row".

"Yes, you did. I'm proud of you. You're a jump roper now, Johnny".

CHAPTER 14

Being in the Moment

"Let me ask you something", said Mr. P. "Why do you think you were able to jump over the rope seven times in a row just now but one minute ago you couldn't do three jumps in a row?"

"Um, let me think. Well, when you asked me to jump over the rope three times, I became scared and worried. I didn't think I could jump over the rope three times in a row. I thought I would make a mistake".

"And what happened?" asked Mr. P.

"I made a mistake. But the next time, I wasn't worried about making a mistake. Almost without thinking, I just kept jumping over the rope, one jump at a time".

"Fantastic, Johnny. You were in the moment".

"I was in the moment. What does that mean?"

"You were not thinking about the past or the future. You did not worry about making a mistake and you didn't care that you made a mistake before. Instead, you just started jumping and you did one jump at a time".

"Yes, that's what I did", I said. "Like, when I'm playing computer games, sometimes I have no time to think, and I just push the buttons and try to make my character do something well".

"Yes, just like that, Johnny. But, to become a really great jump roper, you will have to practice often".

"I will", I said, excitedly.

"I know you will. I believe in you. And, remember, when learning, you will make many mistakes. That's normal, and it's okay to become frustrated. But don't give up. Believe in yourself. Keep practicing. Work hard but have fun and don't worry too much about getting better. If you worry too much, you might not enjoy jumping rope. Just keep practicing and you will get better. Be patient".

"Pay….pay…pay-shint", I said. "What does that mean?"

CHAPTER 15

Patience & Small Improvements

"To be patient means you have time to learn. So, if you make lots of mistakes one day, that's okay because you can try again the next day and the day after that and the day after that".

"There's no hurry to learn", I said. "Is that right?"

"That's right, Johnny. You don't have to make big improvements every day. In life, it's great to have big dreams but focus on making small improvements regularly. If you keep making small improvements, you will achieve big dreams".

"I think I understand. Or, maybe I don't. Can you tell me again?"

"Let me show you", he said.

Mr. P put out his hand, and so I gave him the jump rope.

He started jumping over the rope with his two feet together. Then he started jumping with just one foot. Then he started doing all kinds of amazing moves.

"Awesome!" I said. "That was awesome".

"Pretty awesome, yes. But I didn't learn all these tricks in one day. It took me several years. First, I got good at jumping with my two feet together. Then I learned to jump with one foot. After that, I learned a harder move, and then I learned an even harder move. I did that for many years".

"Ah, I understand. I should just try to get a little better all the time. I don't have to learn everything in one day".

"That's right! Very good, Johnny".

"Can I ask you something Mr. P?"

"Sure, Johnny. It's great to ask questions. We can learn a lot by asking other people questions. What do you want to know?"

"Well, Mr. P, when you walked by the computer room and heard me crying, why did you stop? No one ever stopped before".

"Sometimes, Johnny, people are too busy and have their own problems that they don't see that someone else needs their help. When I heard you crying, it reminded me of when I was your age. During that time of my life, I cried a lot".

"You did?"

"Yes, I did", said Mr. P.

CHAPTER 16

Everyone Cries

"Everyone cries, Johnny. People cry when they are sad, and sometimes they even cry when they are happy".

"When you were my age, why did you cry?"

"I usually cried because I was sad or angry about something".

"What did you do to make yourself feel better?"

"I often ate lots of junk food, but that only helped me feel better for a short time. Eating junk food when I was sad caused me to gain weight, and then I just became more sad".

"How did you change?" I asked.

"Great question! I'm much older now, but I still have problems. Everyone has problems, Johnny".

"They do?"

"Yes, they do. But people often don't talk about their personal problems".

CHAPTER 17

Turn Weaknesses into Strengths

"If everyone has their own problems, why don't people talk about their problems?" I asked.

"Sometimes people feel embarrassed and weak for having problems", replied Mr. P. "But our problems can actually make us become better and stronger".

"They can?"

"Yes, for example, if I am bad at math, I have choices. I could keep saying to myself, 'I'm weak at math'. Or, I could study more and get extra help from my math teacher. If I choose to study more and get help, I will become better at math. You see?"

"Yes, I understand. We all have problems. What's important is what we choose to do about our problems. Right?"

"Exactly right", said Mr. P. "If I'm sad or in a bad mood, I try to do positive things like jump rope or listen to music. Or, I might talk with a friend. In the mornings when I wake up, I'm sometimes tired. To make myself feel better mentally and physically, I listen to music while making coffee. Then I read some pages of a book to exercise my mind, and then I jump rope outside in the fresh air to exercise my body. After that, I shower and have breakfast, and then I feel much better. Does that make sense?"

"Yes, I think I understand. So, during recess and lunch, instead of always coming into the computer room and playing games and eating junk food, I could go outside and jump rope".

"Yes, that could be a great idea", said Mr. P. "But it's also okay to play computer games and eat some candy and junk food. I do that, too".

"You do? Even you?"

"Yes, I enjoy using my computer. I also like watching TV. But I always try to do some exercise every day. Today after school, I will walk around the running track for 20 or 30 minutes before going home".

Mr. P then put his hand in his pocket and pulled out a chocolate bar wrapper.

"I ate a chocolate bar one hour ago", he said. "It was delicious".

We both laughed.

CHAPTER 18

Healthy Habits

"I love candy", Mr. P said. "But I try to eat healthy food most of the time. You see, sometimes when we want to accomplish a goal, such as improving our body shape, we have to stop or reduce some bad habits. So, these days, instead of eating lots of candy and drinking cola, I usually eat fruit and drink water or milk. But I still eat a little candy some days".

"I love chocolate", I said, smiling. "I also like lollipops, licorice, gummies, and caramels".

"Me, too", said Mr. P. "But tomorrow, instead of eating candy, I will have some ants on a log for a snack".

"Do you like eating ants?" I asked, surprised.

Mr. P laughed and said, "Ants? No. *Ants on a Log* is a snack made by spreading peanut butter or almond butter on celery and then placing raisins on top".

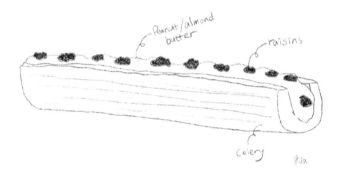

I laughed and said, "Oh, so the raisins are like ants walking on the celery which looks like a log".

"That's right".

"I like raisins and peanut butter, and I like eating celery because it's crunchy. Maybe I can make *ants on a log* with my family".

"Yes, they might enjoy that".

He then continued talking. "When I started eating less junk food, I began to lose body fat and I felt stronger and had more energy. And do you know what else happened?"

"No, what else happened, Mr. P?" I asked, excitedly.

"Because I lost body fat and had more energy, jumping rope became even easier".

"It did?"

"Yes. The first few times I tried jumping rope, I could only jump for a few seconds. I got tired so quickly. But each week, it became easier".

"Each week, you got a little better at jumping rope", I said.

"That's right. Each week, I got a little better. In life, Johnny, it's amazing what you can achieve by doing just a little better every day. After several months, my body shape improved a lot and I could jump rope quite well. I was even able to do some jump rope tricks".

"I want to learn jump rope tricks, too. How did you learn to do tricks?"

"I learned tricks from reading jump rope books. But with the internet, you can watch jump rope videos online".

"I will do that", I said.

"When I did jump rope tricks at school, the other kids thought my jump rope tricks were so cool that they wanted to learn how to do them", said Mr. P.

"They did?"

"Yes. And I think if you jump rope outside at school, other kids will want to try with you".

"They will?"

"I think so".

"That would be so fun", I said, smiling. "Instead of playing by myself in the computer room, I could be outside jumping rope with some of the other kids".

"That sounds nice", said Mr. P.

"I definitely want some friends. But, Mr. P, I get nervous around people. You're a teacher, so you're always around people. How do you not get nervous?"

CHAPTER 19

Getting Nervous is Normal

Mr. P laughed and said, "Johnny, I get nervous, too. Everyone gets nervous. But, what works for me is this: when I'm with other people, I focus on being kind and getting to know them. I try not to worry about what I look like in front of them or whether I might say something silly. Instead, I try to listen closely when they are speaking. People appreciate it when you really listen to them when they speak. It shows that you care about them. I also try to ask questions. Asking questions shows that you are interested in what others have to say. Does that make sense?"

"I think so, yeah".

Mr. P then continued talking. "So, when I'm in the classroom, yes, I get nervous but not too much because my focus is on my students. My main motivation for teaching is how I can best help my students improve. I believe that when you focus on others with kindness and a caring attitude, you become less nervous around others".

"I think I understand, Mr. P. So, for example, if other kids want to jump rope with me, I can focus on helping them learn. I can also listen to them when they speak and ask questions to learn more about them".

"Yes, that's great, Johnny. Of course, you can also talk about yourself. When you talk about yourself or share information about your life with other people, it can make them more interested in you and at the same time they may feel more comfortable telling you information about themselves since you already shared information about yourself".

"I see. Thanks Mr. P."

"You're welcome. Well, Johnny, I have to go now. It was great spending a little time together".

"Thank you Mr. P. Before you go, can I ask you another question?"

"Sure. What do you want to ask me?"

"Well, I wonder, how long do you plan to jump rope for? Will you jump rope forever?"

CHAPTER 20

Staying Active to Live Well

"I wish I could jump rope forever, Johnny. I will jump rope for as long as I'm able to. As we get older, our bodies may not be able to move like they could when we were young. And that's okay. That's a part of life. But, being active when you are young will help your body be strong and healthy as you get older. So, stay active".

"Okay. Mr. P, if you don't mind me asking, how old are you?"

He smiled and said, "I'm 42. But, here's the important thing Johnny, I feel like I'm 22 years old".

"You do?"

"Yes. And I believe that how you feel is more important than your real age. So, my real age is 42, but I feel like I'm 22. And do you know what?"

"What?"

"I try not to worry too much about the future. I try to enjoy myself and do my best each day. If I do that, my future should be fine".

"Yes, I think I understand", I said.

"You do?"

"I think so, yeah. When I get older, I may not be able to jump rope as well as I could when I was a kid, but that's okay. The important thing is to enjoy jumping rope now and to keep having fun and moving my body for as long as I can".

"Exactly, Johnny. That's right! Nothing lasts forever. So, try to enjoy your time now. You're a very smart boy. You have a great future ahead of you".

"I do?"

"Yes. Believe in yourself", said Mr. P.

"Okay, I will try".

CHAPTER 21

One Brick at a Time

"And remember, when you are learning something, just keep trying to make small improvements", Mr. P said.

Then he pointed at the brick wall in the computer room.

"That wall", he said, "was made by putting down one brick at a time".

"One brick at a time", I repeated.

"Yes, Johnny. Getting good at jumping rope and becoming successful in life is like building a brick wall. We get better a little all the time. That's what you do when you play computer games, too, isn't it?"

"What do you mean?"

"When you play a computer game, your goal is to get to the next level, right?" asked Mr. P.

"Yes".

"And each level gets a little harder and harder to pass, don't they?" asked Mr. P.

"Yes, they do".

"But, you never quit, do you?"

"No, I don't".

"In life, Johnny, keep trying to get to the next level in the things you do, just like with a computer game".

"Okay, I will".

"You will become great at jumping rope, and you will do great in life", said Mr. P.

"Thank you", I said, with tears coming out of my eyes.

I was crying again, but this time I was crying because I was happy.

"Bye Johnny".

"Bye Mr. P".

But as he was walking out of the computer room, I noticed I was still holding his jump rope.

"Mr. P! Wait!" I shouted.

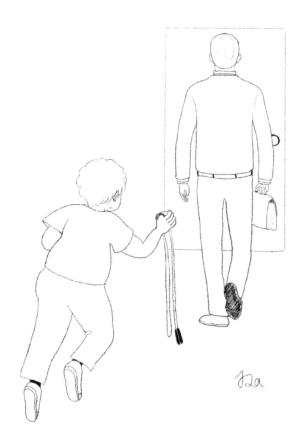

"Yes, Johnny", said Mr. P, as he turned around.

"You forgot your jump rope".

"It is yours now, Johnny. I want you to keep it".

"Really? Thank you, Mr. P. Thank you".

And then he was gone.

CHAPTER 22

Inspire Each Other

That was the last time I saw Mr. P.

Since he was a substitute teacher, he worked at different schools. He never taught at our school again.

But Mr. P changed my life.

I started jumping rope at home almost every day. And each week, I got better and better. I also lost body fat.

Then I began jumping rope at school.

And Mr. P was right. Other kids at school watched me and wanted to try.

We even formed a jump rope club.

And guess who the leader of our jump rope club is? Me!

Everyone at school now calls me *Jump Rope Johnny*. That's my new nickname. No one calls me *Johnny Peter the Eater* anymore. It's so cool.

Our jump rope club members love to jump rope together. And when we make mistakes, sometimes we laugh, but we help each other try to get better.

Sometimes we jump rope while listening to music.

When the weather is good, we jump rope outside in the fresh air and sunshine. We always feel so good when we jump rope outside before going back inside for class.

If it's raining, the school lets us jump rope inside the school gym.

Our school even gave us money to buy extra jump ropes. Aren't we lucky?

And, guess what?

I still play computer games, but now I have friends to play with.

Maybe you would like to join our jump rope club. You might love jumping rope.

If you don't like to jump rope, that's okay, but it's important to have a hobby or many hobbies. Do you know what a hobby is?

CHAPTER 23

Find Hobbies You Enjoy

A hobby is something you do for fun in your free time.

There are so many hobbies you could try. My sister Anne loves taking photographs. My cousin Derek cycles his bicycle. My uncles Johnson and Han play golf. My aunts Eimear and Tina enjoy reading.

How about you? Do you have a hobby?

Mr. P said it's important for kids to try a lot of different activities so they can find things that make them happy and that make their lives more exciting.

I always look forward to jumping rope together with my jump rope club.

So, try many activities. Find things you enjoy. Practice often and you could become great.

When you get better and better at your hobbies, you will gain confidence. If you learn something you didn't think you could learn, that will help you feel good about yourself, and you will believe that you can achieve more and more. It's wonderful.

Oh yeah, do you remember that I told Mr. P that I liked to watch ice hockey?

Well, Mr. P told me to remember that just because a team is losing by many goals doesn't mean they cannot still win the game.

He was right.

CHAPTER 24

Hard Times are often Temporary

Last night, my favorite ice hockey team was losing by 6 goals with only 20 minutes left in the game. But do you know what happened? They scored eight goals and won the game.

So, if you are not happy about something or you have problems in your life or at school, things can get better.

I was often sad and angry. But my life improved and yours can, too.

To improve your life, you might have to change some of your habits and make better choices.

I was overweight because of my habits and the choices I made. Instead of walking to school, I always took the bus. Instead of walking up the school stairs, I used the elevator. Instead of eating things like fruit or yogurt for dessert in the cafeteria, I always ate pies and pastries. Instead of playing outside, I stayed inside and used my phone or the computer.

And one more very important lesson Mr. P taught me when I had no friends is this: he said I should be my own best friend first.

CHAPTER 25

Be Kind to Yourself & Others

Sometimes we treat ourselves badly. We say mean things to ourselves. I used to call myself fat, ugly, and stupid.

I had to change the way I treated myself. Instead of saying negative things to myself, I said positive messages to myself. For example, "I am smart", "I am kind", "I am strong", and "I am brave".

After I started treating myself better, I became more friendly and confident around other people.

Instead of walking down the hallways in school with my eyes looking at the floor, I made friendly eye contact with the other students. And because I was friendlier, they were friendlier to me. Isn't that cool?

So, if we want others to treat us nicely, we have to treat them nicely.

CHAPTER 26

It's Okay to Ask for Help

Mr. P also taught me one final important lesson. He taught me that it's okay to ask people for help. He said asking others for help is a sign of strength and courage, not weakness.

If you are sad or you are having problems, talk with someone. You could talk with a friend, or a family member, or a counselor.

Maybe one of your friends needs your help.

If you share your problems with a friend, they may also share their problems with you.

We can help each other become better.

EPILOGUE

Goodbye for Now

Well, I have to go to class now.

I'm almost finished seventh grade. Can you believe it? Soon, I will be in high school.

I'm a little nervous about high school, but I'm also excited to meet new people. The high school that I will go to has a jump rope club, so I'm looking forward to becoming a member.

I hope you enjoyed reading my story.

Maybe you and I can meet one day and jump rope together.

Your friend,
Jump Rope Johnny

Printed in Great Britain
by Amazon

26324066R00067